In This Place, She is Her Own.

In This Place, She is Her Own. ©2018 by **Holly Day**. Published in the United States by Vegetarian Alcoholic Press. Not one part of this work may be reproduced without expressed written consent from the author. For more information, please contact vegalpress@gmail.com

ISBN: 978-1-7326827-2-6

Acknowledgements

"My Mother's Last Days" appeared in *Free XpresSion Vol. XVI #10*
"Blur" appeared in *Xero Vol. II #3*
"Sunshine on the Rubble" appeared in *Not One of Us #54*
"Washington Coast, Brief Stop" appeared in *Black Moon #2*
"Train to Gainesville" appeared in *Blacktop Passages #2*
"Overhead" appeared in *Star*Line* Vol. 37 #1
"On the Way to California" appeared in *Speer Presents December 1995*
"Grief" appeared in *Borderlands: Texas Poetry Review #40*
"Sunday Morning Miracles" appeared in *California Quarterly* Vol. 37 #4
"The Needle" appeared in *Stand* Vol. 12 #1
"To a Son Leaving Home" appeared in *The Cannon's Mouth* #52
"The Rabbit" appeared in *Exit 13 Magazine #20*
"Museum Display #321" appeared in *Pinyon #19*
"Quiet, Like Marble" appeared in *Gargoyle #62*
"The Unbelievable Sadness of Open Plains Cut By Highways" appeared in *A Journal of Nature Poems* Vol. XII #4
"With Crumbling Foundations" appeared in *Pinyon #19*
"The Fox" appeared in *Trestle Creek Review #20* and *Poets Espresso Vol. 6 #25*
"Thumbelina" appeared in *Extract(s)* Vol. 2
"Metamorphosis" appeared in *New Mirage Quarterly August 2001*
"Censorship" appeared in *SpinDrifter Vol. 1 #1, Pennine Ink #29* and *Real: Regarding Arts & Letters* Vol. 35.1
"Violets" appeared in *Prathmata Samoy* Vol. 1 #1
"Surma" appeared in *Palace Corbie #7, Asspants #6* and *Phoebe Vol. 13 #2*
"Crossing Guard" appeared in *Iota 82*
"Lover" appeared in *Homestead Review* Spring 2016
"Size 8" appeared in *Not One of Us #48*
"The Hatchlings" appeared in *Cold Mountain Review* Vol. 42 #1
"Hands Fold Like Dying Butterflies" appeared in *fourW #25*
"Passacaglia" appeared in *Et Cetera* Vol. 70 #4 and *Neon Literary Magazine #38*
"Some Memories Will Be Left Behind" appeared in *The Cannon's Mouth #52*

Table of Contents

1	With Crumbling Foundations
2	Last Words
3	The Flood
4	Quiet, Like Marble
5	The Sacrifice
6	My Side of the Yard
7	The Unbelievable Sadness of Open Plains Cut by Highways
8	The Dance
9	Morning Walk
10	Convenient Deities
11	Unfinished
12	The Stick
13	With My Daughter
14	Turtles
15	Sunshine on the Rubble
16	The First Attempt
17	In Flight
18	The Things We Keep
19	Escalation
20	Passing
21	On the Way to California
22	The Fourth Voyage
23	My Mother's Last Days
24	The Place of Future Thoughts
25	Another Woman Talking to Herself
26	The Needle
27	Andromeda
28	Faith
29	For New Constellations
30	The Way We Move
31	Scraps
32	Just Making Conversation
33	Censorship
34	Museum Display #321
35	Isolation
36	Crossing Guard
37	A House for Tiny Spirits
38	Some Memories Will Be Left Behind
39	The Unscheduled Interruption
40	The Fox
41	The Hatchlings
42	The Invasion
43	Just In Case
44	Safe
45	Washington Coast, Brief Stop
46	Surma

47	Bonfire
48	With the End of a Pin
49	Blur
50	To a Son Leaving Home
51	An Afternote to a Book Without Us
52	Thumbelina
53	Size 8
54	Achilles
55	How to Move Life
56	After the Fire
57	Poetry
58	The Morning After a Funeral We Didn't Attend
59	Sunday Morning Miracles
60	A Solitary Spot
61	Passacaglia
62	Overhead
63	Too Late
64	Pulling You Away
65	Hypochondriac
66	Train to Gainesville
67	Metamorphosis
68	Dogs
69	The Rabbit
70	The First Step
71	In Wait
72	Grief
73	Hands Fold Like Dying Butterflies

With Crumbling Foundations

we pass each other once, twice a year
my old friends, my getting-older friends
chance encounters at the grocery store, brief escapes
to the bar. we barely recognize each other,
so much time has passed. we fumble with words
to express appreciation for new hairstyles
a recent manicure, minor accomplishments
tiptoeing around the subject
of our obvious physical decay.

buildings and civilizations rise from the dust
flourish and die just outside my house
as I fold laundry, cook dinner
straighten the same damned pillows
again and again, make phone calls
to the outside world, to remind the few people
who still remember me

that I'm still here.

Last Words

where to put the special instructions
that detail what must happen to me when I die?
is this the thing I should have tattooed
on the wide, soft flesh of my inner thigh
or across my chest surrounded by roses and butterfly wings
or just tastefully scrawled across my back, between my shoulder blades
like some arcane biblical phrase or a line from Sanskrit?

who to send the special instructions
who can I trust?
some lawyer receiving a letter through the mail post mortem
the bored children I leave behind interested only in what I've left them
the husband who's just pissed that he didn't die first? I want to be

tucked into the ground in soft white wings, wrapped in my coffin
in the folds of a bat, want my skin stripped away completely my bones
scoured and bleached, want eagles to take my eyes and liver into space
want to be missed.

The Flood

the coffins float to the surface
like rebellious architecture, buoyed by the floodwaters
that have shaken everything loose. we pass sandbags
hand over hand to build a wall between us and the river
shouting panicked instructions to the trucks to bring more.

the water pouring in from the river is frigid and cold
numbing ankles and hands, but the water
running off the bloated cemetery is warm, as though
carrying the last breath and embrace of the dead
across the grounds to keep us from freezing.

Quiet, Like Marble

I remember when I had my own scent, and not that
of the household products I use
and not that of the man I sleep with
and not of the various children and creatures that drool on or lick at me
during the course of the day. I have become
a repository for other creatures' smells
laundry detergent and bleach vapors
my pillow doesn't even smell like me anymore.

in the language of beasts, I no longer exist.
I am no longer me. I have become only
the children who fall asleep in my lap, warm hair twisted and embedded in my clothes
the wet dog that shakes itself off on me after our morning walk
the man who rubs his own scent roughly against my flesh every night--

everything I am is only
an extension of these things.

The Sacrifice

the children respond to their Satanic urges
willingly, stake the sacrifice to the cardboard mat
laugh as it struggles, poke it with the end of a pin. this is not
scientific, their mother warns, shaking her head
in disproval. you have to be merciful.

one more pin and the butterfly stops twitching, opens
its wings one last time and dies, posed like a magazine ad
for wildlife preserves or idyllic Midwestern vacations.
the children back up from their work, admire
the way the sunlight falls on the butterfly's iridescent wings
the way it settles on and illuminates the tiny scales perfectly
almost as if it is still alive.

My Side of the Yard

the leaves catch fire and burst
into flaming insects pouring out from beneath
every smoking leaf and branch
some of them
clutch tiny parcels of white eggs
drag their children from the burning rubble
scream oh god oh god how
did this happen oh god and I

refuse to answer their prayers I flick
another match on the pile and watch as it snaps
immediately into more fire I casually stomp
on a schoolbus full of children old people
streaking from the bonfire as though this

will be their salvation swat at helicopters
bearing important insect politicians to safety
slap at intrepid explorers climbing my shoes my
pant leg as though trying to confront me face-to-face

I have no mercy for any of them I
do not want bugs in my kitchen and this
collection of anthills termite mounds
wasp nests is too close to my house
this is not allowed.

The Unbelievable Sadness of Open Plains Cut by Highways

clouds cover the skies, far off to the west, forever
finding a way to hide what hides just ahead, always
a way to pretend there is always something there, it never ends
the way I see the horizon, so long as I'm standing here.
something screaming clanging far away means here comes
a train a car, full of people full of nothing

caterpillars and bridges

rise and fall like waves, there is always
another road that starts up just where the bottom step ends
the wind lifts the hem of my cotton dress, hold it down at the edge here
and here, with one tiny hand that will someday too long ago turn into an adult hand,
comes
a time when tomorrow and yesterday and nothing
all matter equally, so long as there are bridges

the roads run forever

and every time it seems like the concrete carpaths end, here
comes another, another endless road that leads as far as nothing
beneath the bridges where the water runs to forever
in the middle of nowhere, sometimes even always isn't enough.

The Dance

you've finally caught her, across the room, promises of
fairy tale castles and big screen love-
scenes in your eyes—I remember being her, once
in the days before I became a rotting corpse
waiting by the telephone, in the dark,
in our bed, always waiting for you
to come back home.

one last pastel-colored cocktail and she is yours for
ever, or just tonight, whatever you decide her role will be.
she glides through the walls of human flesh
toward you as if summoned, and here,
far away, I know exactly what you are
thinking, lying here, rotting from my hollow places
begging for just one last bite
from your hard, sharp axe,
before you
plow me under.

Morning Walk

the turkey spreads its great wings, stares down at me
small, bald head blue against its ruff of black feathers
opens its mouth to chirp questioningly at me
reluctant to leave its roost in the tree.

the dog pulls at her leash and barks at the bird, who answers
by spreading its massive wings even wider. It leaps into the air, wobbles, clumsy
as if just learning to fly, somehow pulls that immense body
up into the sky.

Convenient Deities

the god of the bus stop tells me it's going to rain today, reminds me
that I have an umbrella under my desk at work, reminds me
that I'm trying to quit smoking. in the days before
the bus stop god moved in and chased away the other riders
the occasional sleeping bum, I used to smoke
a half a pack a day, but I don't anymore.

the god of my office has already set my umbrella out for me, apparently tipped off
by the god of the bus stop, or perhaps some random weather god
I haven't met yet, has already removed the spare change from my desk drawer
so that I won't be tempted to go buy a couple of cigarettes
from the smokers in the warehouse during my lunch break. I have
just enough money in my pocket for the bus ride home, and I thank the bus stop god
for leaving me with that.

at home, the god of my apartment
lets me know how many times the electricity flickered on and off
due to faulty wiring that my landlord really should fix
and how many times he saved my apartment from filling with gas
from my stove's extinguished pilot light, lets me know
my cats are safe with him in my home, that
I need to do my laundry soon.

Unfinished

he started the book and the leaves curled to embrace him
sent tendrils in curlicues to bind his wrists, insisting
it's only a book, years later
he's still watering its pages and feeding it flies.

inside the man bloomed a story that wouldn't die
grew helplessly parasitic and devoured his days
to the consternation of neighbors who shook their heads at his dreams
talked about how his roof was falling apart.

The Stick

if you hammer a stick into the ground, will it grow into a tree? will it
stretch splinters into roots, cover itself with new bark
grow high into the air and spread branches like wings
disappear into the canopy overhead and make room only
for tropical birds?

and if that stick is really a spear, will the metal point
disappear into the heart of the new tree, a dormant weapon
waiting for the right king to come along to pull it out
just in time to give his faltering cause absolution
or will it simply disintegrate into the corrosive sap of the tree
become black and twisted before breaking into dust?

With My Daughter

crows and starlings scatter at the shotgun crack of the ice
shifting and splintering into blue-gray shards.
there is water running in the falls again, a thin trickle
moving beneath the snow
just enough to break through thoughts of winter.

we stand on the bank of the creek, hand in hand, as we've done
every winter since she was born, watching the ice shake loose
in great, heavy sheets, crashing like thunder
on the rocks below.

Turtles

at the far end of the pond, a family of ducks
makes its way across the water. the mother duck
cuts quickly towards the safety of the tall cattails
as if aware of the danger stalking her brood.

as I watch, first one, then another yellow duckling
are pulled beneath the surface, so fast
it might be some sort of duck magic trick.
the mother duck plunges grimly ahead
the remaining brood close behind.

by the time she reaches the far shore, there are only two babies
left to follow. She slows her retreat and urges them forward
into the shadow of exposed willow roots, the safety of the shallows,
eyes fixed on the depths where her other children disappeared.

Sunshine on the Rubble

we approach each other's present-day
as civilizations in decline, look beyond
the conquered walls and shattered windows
scars carved in flesh by unmentionable acts
remnants of wars that must be acknowledged
but written and spoken only as
fixed, immutable points in the past.

instead, we revel in the struts left standing
despite the damage, point out the fine detailing
in frescoed hallways and ornamental lintels
find beauty in even the most accidental of places:

a line of tiny flowers blooming in a sidewalk crack
a spray of green lichen obscuring decades of decay
a statue of a girl I used to be, still standing guard
over the last of the locked doors
I will open only for you.

The First Attempt

the baby gorilla lies on the table
tiny, furry arms spread like an angel's. so much
was supposed to happen here that won't.

in the other room, the new mother chews thoughtfully
on an orange, spitting the seeds out loudly
against the far wall. she does not like seeds. before her

is a tower of offerings: a cluster of small, bruised bananas
oranges, kiwis, sliced apples with the cores removed
all brought by caretakers whose hearts have been broken.

In Flight

I wake up and he's still gone, he's still
all grown up and gone. my husband rolls over and glares
"what?" at me, he knows I'm thinking about
our son, he's been gone a whole week and I've
only heard from him twice.

I go into the kitchen and make
too much food, cook things the way my son likes
but his sister doesn't. "I don't like my eggs
this way," she says, pushing her plate away.
"eat your fucking eggs," growls my husband
glaring at me.

all day long, I think about him
almost pick up the phone to call and shout
"where are you? are you okay?
do you want to come home?" but I don't
because I know I'm not supposed to.
my heart curls up on itself
like a tiny, crippled bird in my chest
and only time will set it right.

The Things We Keep

my son asks me for a notebook for school
and without thinking, I hand him one
from my office, because most of the notebooks
I keep in there are empty.

later, I find my poems crumpled in the bathroom trashcan
ripped out of a notebook obviously
not empty. I pull the poems out of the trash
smooth out the wrinkles, wonder

at this relationship between mother and child
where only one party is duty-bound to crow over each
submitted piece of art, each small accomplishment
expecting no similar response in return.

Escalation

if I lay still enough
long enough
on the hard-packed snow, on the frozen mud and ice
will my body warm up the ground enough
to trick the tiny seeds
into thinking that it's spring?

if we lie here together
on the same patch of earth
will our combined heat
wake crocuses, make snowdrops unfurl
shake Christmas roses awake
convinced that it's spring?

if you make love to me, here, in the snow
will our bodies melt
enough of this tundra
to make tulips and daffodils race up
through the mud
open bright crowns to herald
an early arrival of spring?

Passing

another letter comes from you
and the space between each letter's arrival
folds up and disappears as if we've been
engaged in constant conversation this whole time. I wish

I could stack those silent spaces into a drawer
put them away, forget them completely
so that I could be as young as I was
when we first started communicating this way.

or even younger, like when we still lived close to one another
pressed close in the hallway at school
had actual conversations that didn't require
assembling a variety of loose postage stamps.

On the Way to California

you tell me there is sanctuary in Ogallala
among the dreams of dead whores in the Midwest's Gomorrah
a place where we can cocoon before the red eyes of a coal stove
and no one will wonder
why we never go outside

we could share a sleeping bag in front of the fireplace
listen to the tom cat howl of the cold wind outside
play blind finger games, "oh your skin is so warm"
and no one will call
to lure us to church

you tell me of wagon trains stopped on the plains
cattle nomads tired of endless west
gunslingers and movie scripts and coal miners and housewives
where no one asks questions
people leave you alone

The Fourth Voyage

we cut the ship loose and set it off towards the icebergs. its hull
scraped against the sharp edges as it passed. jagged white chunks fell off
on both sides of the deck. *we can't keep everything,* you said.
not even our memories, but I wasn't listening
determined to hold onto the moment
because I do intend to keep some things for myself.
maybe everything.

we turned and made our way up into the cliffs, looking for the perfect place
to build a new home. I longed for the deck of the long-gone ship
tossing in the waves far below, the comfort of the tiny, enclosed cabin
wondered at our hastiness and the hazards of free will. but there are rocks all around us
enough, you say, to pile into a castle, an apartment complex, a village
a single, tiny hovel for us to spend the rest of our misguided days.

My Mother's Last Days

I slip the bracelet into my pocket
try the ring on my finger
catch myself in the mirror
see her sleeping behind me.
my mother is sick.

at home, I empty my purse out, my pockets
put the jewelry in a drawer
of photographs and dried corsages.
someday she'll be gone

too soon.

The Place of Future Thoughts

a crazy lady who says she's my mother is giving a lecture on dark matter
to a large group of crazy ladies in the other room, all of which
claim to be scientists of some sort or another, which worries me because
I know for a fact they are not scientists. the lady who says she's my mother waves
a piece of paper in my face, says she's even written a paper
on the subject, on dark matter
it's supposed to prove to me that she's serious. she says her other scientist friends
are very interested in her revelations on the universe, of the origins of myth
on the paths stretching into the past and future of humanity
but she won't let me read what she's written.

upstairs are two children who are supposed to be mine, and I wonder
how much of the nodding and agreeing that goes on in my house
is simply to placate my own insanities and inanities. the lady who is my mother
wonders why I don't speak up more in crowds, in groups
why I don't share my own theories about the relationships between
the opening of tiny flowers in the morning and the art of trephination
the sound of lightning and the invention of the wheel
with more people, how come if she's brave enough to speak her thoughts out loud

why I keep my own ravings so still and quiet.

Another Woman Talking to Herself

overcome with regret, she cradles him in her arms
before reluctantly devouring his headless corpse. later, she will lay
a clutch of white, oval eggs, knowing
someone else's daughters will eat her own sons someday.

the mantis has no voice for her sorrow, her grief at the loss
of her brief love affair. the crickets take up her song instead
a chorus of chirps that fills the night with shadows.

The Needle

if you could play your fingerprints
with a phonograph needle
what do you think your song would be? is there
an SOS of pops and snaps
in the ridges of your thumbs
or is there an overture waiting to be heard
buried in the whorls of your index finger?

if you could play your skin like a slab
of mint vinyl, would your flaws resound joyous
in bagpipes and flutes, would your wrinkles sound like the ocean
would your calluses rock hard? or would it all be a mess

some unlistenable cacophony
a recording of your failures
silent angers
old age?

Andromeda

they only ask girls to sacrifice themselves
only chain virgins to rocks. if they were to ask
a grown woman, worn down by children
already tiring of life,
already used to settling for less than the stuff of her dreams
it wouldn't really be a sacrifice.
it would just be one more unpleasant chore
something to get through during the course of a day.
"of course I'll do it," that tired woman would say.
"just let me finish up here and I'll be right out."

monsters mean different things
to girls and women. for one
there's the terrifying possibility of being devoured
physically or spiritually, the end of great plans
great dreams. for the other, the chance to meet a monster
is a break from monotony, the happy realization
that the unexpected does still exist outside
the four walls of a day.

Faith

out in my garden are flowers, coiled like springs
waiting to unfurl from the soil
fill my garden with song. I know they're underfoot
beneath the ice and the snow
because I have faith.

if you ask me to explain myself, I can tell you
about how every spring, the maple out front
sends thousands of fluttering seeds into the air
most of which end up in the gutter
while hundreds more get raked into the compost pit

but one or two almost become trees. This will go on
until my venerable maple dies, or until I'm too old
to bend over to pull errant saplings out of my flower bed.
I don't really know anything other than this.

For New Constellations

if you were to set me free, I would leave with only
a rolled-up animal skin tent strapped to my back
a pocketful of dried berries and reindeer meat
a chunk of ice in a bucket to later melt into water.
I would give you one backwards last glance,
one last chance to stop me
before disappearing into a landscape of glaciers and polar bears
a sky filled with so many stars.

it would only take moments for my retreating figure
to be swallowed up in an expanse of white snow, only moments
for the wind to erase my footprints, the twin snaky signatures left by my sled.
eventually, you'll discover that all of your letters
have been forwarded to a research station abandoned by Russians
years before, everything you forgot to say in person
has been shredded into bedding by arctic foxes and penguins
chewed into mulch by inquisitive polar bears.

The Way We Move

I gave in to you in an exhale of broken pinfeathers, the soft snarl of a cornered coyote
some fragile, trapped thing trying to chew its own foot off, determined to live on
with a broken, bloodied stump for a paw. you were oblivious to the struggle
saw only instead the dead weight I would add to your already painful burden.

this house has become a tiny raft on a rough river, a barricade
against some kind of reality, a fire-wielding mob,
the phone calls that come in the middle of the night
that may or may not signal the death of someone important to one or both of us.
there is no time for love here. we don't speak of how much time we'd need.

Scraps

the fly lands on the edge of my sandwich
stands on four legs, rubs its front two together
as if about to break into song
break out a set of tiny silverware
break into some used-car-salesman lecture
that'll make me give it my whole sandwich
maybe go make it another whole sandwich
to take home to its family.

I swat impatiently at the fly, send it off
without waiting to hear it sing, or speak,
or beg, because I have heard
that flies either shit or puke on food they want to eat
they do something disgusting to it, and I
don't want to think about it. instead
I rip the corner of the sandwich the fly was on
toss it to the grateful dog sitting patient in the corner
also watching me eat.

Just Making Conversation

it's strange how we all have so many of the same parts inside of us.
we have lungs and a heart just like a squirrel's, a digestive system that looks
indistinguishable from a pig's. if you were to gut a pig and a man next to one another
in the morning, you wouldn't be able to tell which pool of rusty-red dried blood
came from which creature. if you slit a goat or a dog or a rabbit from neck to navel
all of the organs fall out in the same sort of bundle, just a different-sized bundle.

I don't know what I'm telling you this for, but you decided
that the empty seat next to me was some sort of invitation to conversation.
if you don't want to talk about the things I like talking about, perhaps
you should find another drinking companion.
I could tell you something about the steer that lost his hide
to make these leather pants I'm wearing, tell you all about the things
that lived in the trees cut down
to make this here bar we're drinking at,
but I can tell you're the type of guy who likes simpler stories than these.

Censorship

I fold sheet after sheet of the Sunday paper
under the top, determined to hide the words
"troops" and "dead" and "war" from
my son's curious eyes. "can I have the funnies?"
he asks, and I scan the section carefully to see
if he can read them safely today.

we pass the morning talking about
robots and aliens and orange tabby cats
and he tells me he's going to be an astronaut someday
and says I can ride in his spaceship
any time. I move my coffee cup to hide the words
"biological warfare" and tell him
I've always wanted to see the stars
up close.

Museum Display #321

if, instead of dogtags, these men had each left behind
a single shoe, a hat, a glove, this room
would overflow in memoriam.
there would be no space left for casual viewing
for museum passersby to stop and read
the tiny letters that spell out
loss.

there are suitcases of song and memory
attached to each silver tag, buried somewhere
behind faraway churches
beneath the settling foundations of houses
in farmlands tilled with the rising sun
surrounded by field mice
still curled in sleep.

Isolation

when I first moved to Mexico, I knew just enough Spanish
to buy groceries, say hello to my neighbors
to tell telemarketers I couldn't speak Spanish. I knew
three people who could speak English: two of them were
unfriendly, catty women, a little older than me, and an old man
named Roberto who preferred his cat to people. for one

whole month, I was surrounded by a world
that could not talk to me, and it was bliss.

one day, Roberto showed up at the door with his daughter.
she was my age, he said, and he thought we should be friends.
"we will teach you Spanish," he said. "you'll learn from both of us."
every day, the two of them would bring me cookies and fruit for breakfast,
I would make coffee, and Roberto would tirelessly
give me the words for the things around me.

I didn't know how to tell him I had come here for silence
that I was happiest when I had no idea what was being said.

within a year, the murmur of voices in the streets
became real conversations, the excited sportscasters on TV
made complete sense, I could hold conversations
with strangers. Roberto's daughter and I had nothing in common—
she loved shopping and boys, I liked drugs and punk rock.
they eventually stopped coming by for breakfast

but the damage had been done. the world made sense again
and I was no longer alone.

Crossing Guard

the crossing guard waits
until the children are out of sight
before removing his head.

his eyes close as he does so,
lips go slack
pale.

I think I could be happy
if I could remove my head
get rid of my sad, heavy brain,
savaged by electricity
silly little pills.

I can never tell
if he can see anything without his head
so I wave to him from my window,
just in case.

A House for Tiny Spirits

when I die, trap my soul in a birdcage
with a little plastic bath, and a plastic bowl for food
wrap the bars in cellophane so I can't slip through

because I will never be ready to go.

I will learn all the right songs to convince your guests
that it's a bird in the cage, and not your dead wife
I will finally learn how to whistle in key.

Some Memories Will Be Left Behind

he leans in to kiss me and I suddenly wonder
if this is the memory that will sustain me
haunt me
when my brain goes to putty, will I be stuck
in an endless loop of this restaurant, his hands,
the sun shining so bright outside it turns
the sidewalks and dirty streets white—
will this be so important to a future me
that it will become the only thing I have left?

and if this doesn't work out, if we don't work out
will this memory seem, at first, jangled
out of place
not worth taking over my final, awful days? will this man
seem a stranger to a dying me, leaning in for this first kiss
over and over again, obliterating
the faces of my someday-husband, someday-children—
this man, will I be able to even remember
his name?

The Unscheduled Interruption

we line up for the photographer, try to look smart and sophisticated,
worthy of observing. there's no telling what one of us might accomplish someday.
there may be a reason for this picture to hang in some important building
in some university hallway, over the desk of an obsessed scholar.
there might be inspiration in our ranks, some yet-undiscovered genius.

we make allowances for an ill-fitting jacket, a stain on a tie, claim
these defects are honest and representational, hide our embarrassment
at being photographed less-than-perfect. someday, when this photograph
is discovered in a stack of loose papers, or hiding under a floorboard
or floating, burned and almost unrecognizable, in a puddle of oily water
no one will notice the elbow patches on a threadbare jacket, the last-minute comb-overs,
the uncomfortable, unaccustomed grin. will the observers of this photo even know who
we are

and if so, will they love or revile us for the things we have yet to do?

The Fox

she is white against the snow and I want her
want to touch the silver fur that slides through imaginary
fingers
like soft spikes of thin mercury, liquid,
more oil than actual air.
her nose quivers black and tiny, sees me
she almost
disappears.

blood red in the snow
where her foot landed—back home, the traps are all sprung
tufts of white fur glow bright
on rusted metal teeth.

The Hatchlings

it unfurls from its egg, fish messiah
spreads translucent fins wide and sails into the river.
behind it, siblings follow suit, tentatively abloom in the water
follow the first-born's gospel of escape.

years from now, when all but a handful have survived
this one moment will be sharp in their subconscious:
a song of rebirth in the raspy breath of the wind
the pull of the current against their new flesh.

The Invasion

the caterpillar crawls along the leaf, a promise of butterflies
thwarted. rough, orange knobs cover its back, a rash of wasp eggs
laid just days before. at any moment

wasp larvae will hatch and split through the caterpillar's soft, emerald skin
tumble clumsily across its helpless body, devour it slowly
until only a dead, empty husk remains.

Just In Case

if one was not familiar with this part of Kansas, one might suspect
that the women here long for summertime all year long. one might mistake
the gigantic, bright-colored butterflies adorning the faded houses
their wingspans reaching over three feet across at times

as an homage to the real butterflies so rarely seen this far from the countryside
fondly remembered by those who grew up on farms, or old enough to recollect
that once there was not a town here. they might not suspect that the gigantic butterflies
are there to both hide great swaths of peeling exterior paint and as a tribute

to a transmorphic deity who also emerged from a cocoon of flesh
whose name is whispered constantly under breath
by huddled housewives convinced the end is coming at any moment.

Safe

we wrap ourselves in plastic and bubblewrap
to avoid splintering on one another.

we layer the masks and blinders on
so we can make it through the day without incident.

there is blood under every step, trauma around every corner
carnage of butterflies and innocents in every breath exhaled.

Washington Coast, Brief Stop

sunset. seabirds land en masse
pick through clumps of bleached seaweed
corn chip bags, half-eaten hot dogs
candy, cookies, popcorn, fruit
sticky and covered with mud. two gulls
make a game of passing orange peels
back and forth, six feet
above the ground.

low tide. silver wraiths flop helpless
on the wet sand, bodies rolling
down the new beach, clumsy,
out of their element. moonlight
picks up scavengers running low
against the sand, field mice
from across the road, raccoons
from the woods next door.

Surma

we identify each other
by our ceremonial tattoos
ritualistic burnings—in the dark
I feel the spot where someone dared you
to put a cigarette out
your fingers brush the jagged 'x'
that was supposed to stop my breath

anthropologists, we explore
each other's damaged pasts
the keloid I got in ninth grade
making happy faces with a lighter, the circle of blue dots
a twelve-year-old did with a safety pin and India ink
the Braille graffiti of your chest
ribs shattered and warped, a mangled child
and a drunk stepfather--we are never

completely naked

Bonfire

the books burn quickly, fill the air with the burning
of tiny insects and mildew spores, ancient glue
and cracked leather. words glow bright on pages
before paper catches fire, being of a more conductive medium.

you can almost read the stories as they explode with light, if you
could just freeze the moment of time between the pages first heating up
and finally catching fire. in the dark, large-print titles flash
briefly, incompletely, before shuddering into monochrome piles of ash.

With the End of a Pin

the spider in my office has left me
another carefully-wrapped parcel of tiny white eggs.
I gently unwrap the webbing from the sac to see
if there is something new to find this time but
it really is
just eggs.

she watches me from the corner of the room
gauging my response to receiving
more eggs from her, and I, in turn
express both surprise and gratitude at the gift. I wonder
at her insistence of giving me the exact same thing
every single time,

but I try not to dwell too much
on the motivation of spiders.

Blur

here can you picture
yourself in old overalls
riding a lawnmower
fixing the sink can you

imagine waking up
in the middle of the
night to challenge
the thing in the kitchen

that sounds like a
burglar naked, you lie
next to me in the dark
can you see us tomorrow
or ten years from now

To a Son Leaving Home

he tells me
the world has gotten so small
that even if he gets swallowed up
by the trees in the Amazon
by the heights of Nepal or Kilimanjaro
by the noise of icebergs crashing somewhere past Alaska
he will be able to call me on his cell phone
I can see his face on my computer
I can reach him
any time I want.

I want to tell him
that even the smallest places
can feel gigantic and empty when you're all alone
that even as close as a telephone call might make us feel
we'll still have to hang up sometime
that every minute I don't hear his stereo playing in the basement
that I don't trip over his laundry in the hallway
that I don't hear him rummaging around in the kitchen
I'll wonder how he's doing, if he's okay
if he remembers
how much he is loved.

An Afternote to a Book Without Us

cockroaches raced along the ground here long before
there were dark alleys and rancid dumpsters
truck drivers and greasy spoon diners, old hamburger wrappers
to curl up inside. before we were here, cockroaches
scuttled in the nests of dinosaurs, fed on the sticky albumin
of newly-hatched eggs, dug tunnels in massive piles of fecal matter,
were old even then. they lived through
the asteroids, the second and third great extinctions
left petrified footprints in the mud
alongside our first bipedal ancestors.

they will be here to see the last flower of humanity
wilt in the heat of cataclysm, will polish our bones
with their tiny, patient mandibles, will lay their eggs
in our shirt pockets and empty hats. there will be
no great cockroach takeover,
no post-apocalyptic ascension to superiority—
they will always just *be*, chitinous wings fluttering
scurrying, squeaking in the dark.

Thumbelina

I once was a woman
who prayed and prayed
for just one little baby
maybe a girl
but when the baby finally came
it came much too soon
she was only two inches long
and so quiet

I held my daughter
curled tiny in my palm
begged her to breathe
begged her to move
said I'd make her a cradle out of a walnut shell
and a goose feather for a quilt
if she would just give me a sign
some sign that we could be

I spent all night by the window, sang lullabies
murmured half-remembered nursery rhymes
my daughter cupped in the palm of my hand
too small to be
anything but a dream.

Size 8

I will know I have lived a good life
when everything I own
at the time of my death
can fit into a shoebox
you can slip under the bed

so when you want to talk
or just remember
you can reach down beneath the covers
and pull all of me out
the poems, our rings
the last good photographs
of the two of us together

we can always be together.
I won't take up much room.

Achilles

drawn to the things we know
will hurt us, we call it taking a chance
destiny. we are all as destructible
as mattresses fresh from the factory
purchased so from a showroom without the extra charge of a plasticine dip,
because we know we're more careful than the salesperson implies
only to have the sharp, metal springs poke through the fabric cover
worn thin from sweat and expulsed breast milk
just a few scant years later.

the Greeks delighted in stories of fate
heroes dragged to destiny to the port or city
they were told at birth to never ever visit
on pain of death, but yet
by the end of the story, the hero
lies in the dirt at Troy, an arrow through his heel
or pulling his eyes out on a dusty mountain path
or sprawled out on a rock for wolves to disembowel.

How to Move Life

I feel the pills shudder through my bones
pull the blankets up to my chin. I hear myself talking
from far away, telling my daughter how she needs to turn my head
if I vomit in my sleep, how important it is
that I don't choke on my tongue. I think she thinks
it's some kind of joke, and when I wake up clear-headed, hours later,
I hope she thinks it was all just a joke.

without meaning to, I am constantly frightening my family
with vague threats of running away, of disappearing
into some forest or jungle or into the tunnels that run under the city
and I don't mean to, the words just slip out
like roaches or spiders bottled up behind my tired lips
an exhalation of rotten air meant to be saved for the dark.

After the Fire

the sun comes up on the wreck of parrots
lights the low-hung clutter of branches.
javelins snuffle out rot in the underbrush, noisy as labor pains
in the silence left in the wake of ruin.

we stalk heavy through the avian Nagasaki
upturning sticky clods of diseased birds with the toes of our boots
wings spread like headdresses in European paintings of Aztecs
bright swaths of blue and yellow wasted in a sea of greasy ash.

Poetry

the dog works long into the night
filling pages with paw prints and psalms
love poems and long strands of dirty drool.
morning is coming and it's
time to eat.

the dog sniffs the new wet leaves covering the sidewalk
thinks of a story it wants to write.
its owner waits patiently as the dog
defecates both out of need and of boredom.
this is what's expected of it
this is what it does.

the dog spends its day trying
to speak to a cat
that refuses to learn a common language
or even share a little of its own.
a small girl says, "good dog," pats it on the head
it knows what that means but wants
so much more.

The Morning After a Funeral We Didn't Attend

I found her the next morning, feeding stacks of old birthday cards
handwritten letters into the paper shredder. "he never loved me," she said
by way of explanation, calmly feeding the first of a pile of faded photographs
into the shredder as I watched. "there's bacon in the kitchen."

I tried to reach out to stop her hand from pushing more and more
of my grandfather into the metal shears that were snipping him down to nothing
but it was her father first, my grandfather second, what right did I have?
"he loved you," I said, watching helpless
as a picture of a blond-haired girl in pigtails
holding onto the outstretched darker hand of a man
fell into the metal waste basket in irretrievable strips.
she laughed and waved a thick handful of bills at me

justification for erasing her father so completely.
"how do you write someone you love out of your will?" she asked.
"why is my stepsister getting everything? he even forgot about *you*!"
I almost said something about
how she hadn't visited her father for years, while her stepmother's family
had been a constant in his life up to the end,
how maybe there wasn't anything left
after the nursing home and the hospice, but I don't, because
that's my father's job.

Sunday Morning Miracles

my son thinks I'm amazing
because I can catch
the tiny spotted toads that swarm the riverbank
with my bare hands

he runs after them as they
retreat into the long wild grasses
smacking his hands together as he
tries to anticipate where they'll jump next

I reach down
slip my fingers under their fragile velvet bodies
and pluck them from the cool green stones
of cattail rushes, find their hiding places
every time, like magic

remembering myself
at his age
I'm a little surprised at the ease of it all
myself

A Solitary Spot

you can't hold a conversation with ice, or the horizon
or the open pools of water that constantly shift and freeze underfoot
depending on how dark the night is
depending on how long the winter lasts. you can't trick the sun
into staying in the same room as you are, no matter how much you need the light
no matter how much you need to feel its brief warmth on your skin.

there can be brief, mostly unrequited conversations
with the hordes of grasshoppers and mosquitoes
that come with the unfolding of wildflowers, the clumps of blue grass
that fill in the brown patches left by winter.
in these moments, you, who have been here the whole time
have become the intruder, inciting suspicious rasps from passing seagulls
the off-kilter dinging of a buoy lost at sea
the stomp of caribou determined to claim Spring for themselves.

Passacaglia

I trudge from the bedroom to the kitchen every morning, hands ready
to make food, fix clothing, brush hair. there is no questioning
my role in this dance, which steps I must take—the required pirouettes
are worn into the carpet as visibly as if someone had outlined my feet in chalk.

the school bus leaves and I turn once, twice, fetch the newspaper from the stoop,
go inside, make coffee. the birds outside the kitchen window watch me move
imitate my pathetic shuffle on the lip of the bird feeder, mock me
with their fluttering wings, their tiny, sure feet, their perfectly coiffed feathers.

I long to find the recordings that dictate my moves
the slow-paced funereal march that decides my day.
I don't know what I'd do with them
except make them stop.

Overhead

the whales could fly simply because
they didn't know they couldn't. off the coast
of Nova Scotia, a swarm of them ascended into the sky
over the tiny fishing villages and bed-and-breakfasts
blotting out the sun in one giant fluttering cloud
of blue-gray tailfins and flashing silver bellies.

it was believed that they would only fly
over the ocean, since that's where they lived
it was hoped that they would stick to waterways that could handle
the weight of a suddenly-gravity-bound cephalopod
but not, fearless, the airborne pods flew inland
disrupted avian migration routes and grounded
hundreds of commuter planes.

eventually, it was accepted as an ordinary day when one could look overhead
and see beluga whales cavorting with sparrows
following great flocks of speckled starlings to Africa and back
to see great blue whales covered with roosting egrets and crowned cranes
or the occasional clumsy dolphin or narwhal learning to fly
curious to see what all the fuss was about.

Too Late

if we were alive a thousand years ago
the only way we would have ever gotten together
would be briefly, you, emerging from your spartan
clay-floored monk's cell, horsehair-stippled habit
hiding your rough, angry frame as you stomp
off into the woods, into the night

to my tiny hut packed with bottles of bright-colored rocks
roof fallen inward from the weight of birds' nests and ivy
packed to the ceiling with things found on my walks
eyes of tiny creatures watching from every corner.
I would greet you at the door, hair wild and unkempt
leaves and twigs stuck in the knots at the base of my neck
greet you and your rules and order without question or thought.

there would be a moment in all of this where we made total sense
where our differences didn't matter, as if we evened each other out
where our grunting and screaming was some type of language
that erased the whole world around us. eventually, though,
just like now..
the sun always comes up
and we remember who we are.

Pulling You Away

you always leave the door open
when you're plotting suicide: poised dramatically in your room
head back, razor against your neck
the sun in the window behind your profile, frozen in time
parting note carefully typed out on your desk.
I scamper down the hallway just in time to giggle
"no, Daddy! don't do it!" as I chase after the cat
who says nothing in protest.

later, you come into my room
sit at the foot of my bed, tell me serious things
about life and work and you and my mother
that I don't understand, speak slow and earnest
promise things I already know you don't mean.

Hypochondriac

she had perfect teeth, possibly because
she never ate anything complicated, eschewed anything too spicy
or heavy, or foreign, as she would never say aloud
but we both knew what she meant when she watched me cook
from the corner of her tiny kitchen, a room
that had seemed so much bigger when I was young.

she left Kansas only twice: once, when she and my grandfather
went to the Dakotas for their honeymoon, a weekend spent
mostly watching her foreign surroundings
through the windows of their rattling Ford and then from behind
the safety of a glass picture window of the tiny lodge
she had spotted and picked out as perfect from the pages of a travel brochure
only to find it completely surrounded by trees and too much wilderness,

the second time, when she went to Colorado to get her lungs x-rayed
looking for the cancer she insisted was there but no doctor could find
despite repeated scans and ultimately devastating biopsies. I've always wondered
if she had known that it was the doctor's tiny, sterile punch holes
that would bring her closer and closer to death, if she
would have gone in again and again, complaining of
shortness of breath, restless nights, repeated and obviously prophetic

dreams of black thunder clouds growling in her chest, malignant
fingers branching like tree limbs in both lobes
things she spoke of often as if preparing us
for her death.

Train to Gainesville

it's very hard to cut yourself on a moving train
without doing real damage. even though the shocks

on most city express trains are pretty decent, there's still flotsam on the tracks,
bits of broken concrete, dead cats and dogs

bumps in the road that cause the cars to sway just enough
to turn what should have been a single straight, hairline crack, just enough

to let out the pressure

into a crazy spurting hole that looks like the result of a back alley knife fight
a mugging gone horribly wrong. you have to choose your canvas

carefully, the tough skin on the top of your leg
the area right above where your shoe ends, some place

easily hidden. the inside of your thigh, that long, white stretch of inviting flesh
is not a good place to cut on a train, it's too soft, goes too fast

too messy and prone to accidental rending. that's the spot you save
for home, with the lights down low, no curious onlookers trying to decipher

what you're doing with your hands underneath your open notebook.

Metamorphosis

I am almost gone. thin fibers
suck the flesh from my body and I
am almost new. cotton fills my
mouth and I don't need to breathe
anymore.

sunlight comes through cracks in the
weave. memories of green and hunger
then they are gone. I am almost
gone. new dreams find their way and it
is almost done.

there are too many stories to live
in such a short time. I speak of two,
maybe three days to go. months spent
fumbling and such a short time to
fly. I break the bindings that keep me
and spread my wings.

Dogs

sometimes I wish I was a dog
and I could jump and kiss and chew on brand new friends
that I didn't have to restrain myself
contain myself to handshakes
polite nods

and I wish I was a dog so I could properly express
the explosive joy trapped in my heart most days
that I could leap and bounce and snap at the air
instead of curt smiles, polite "I'm doing well, thank you"
socially acceptable expressions of happiness.

The Rabbit

I'm trying to write a poem about
the rabbit in my yard. I tell the rabbit
to slow down, stop running, I just
want to sit and write about it for a couple of minutes
about how it looks nibbling on my crocuses and tulips
its tiny, stumpy ears quivering in the early-morning sunlight

but it keeps running away. I have gotten so dirty
crawling across the yard after it, the ground
damp and muddy from melted snow and fresh rain
it won't stop. My notebook in one hand,
a pen tucked behind my ear
I shout after the rabbit, now at the other end of the yard
tell it to slow down, to wait for me, I only have
a couple of questions.

The First Step

I take the piece of paper, put it
in my mouth, feel the word *love* dissolve in my saliva, in my blood
and now I understand marriage.

the individual letters drift like little stones
throughout my body, break up like tiny meteors, turn to sand
sink to my feet and

keep me here.

In Wait

I wrap my thoughts around the egg inside me
tie my nest with hopes and dreams
will my body full of feathers
fluff and bubblewrap.

each step leads me to disaster. I
could trip and fall and lose it all.

I wrap myself in blankets and pills
cradle my stomach in warmth
close windows against drafts and rain
barricade the door against wolves outside.

Grief

this woman claims she's my mother. she dumps her purse out
on the coffee table in front of me, pulls loose, crinkled photos of
small blond children out of the piles of unwrapped tampons with applicator wands
crumbled dollar bills, fuzzy peppermint candies, handfuls of shiny pennies
shows the photos to me and says that they're me, that's me in the picture,
that's my cat.

I tell her I have a mother, that my mother also has a purse full of crap
a purse full of photos of me when I was small, she should go away now.
she waves the photos of a small child holding a giant orange cat in my face and shouts,
"this is your fucking cat! does your other mother have a picture of you and this cat?"
I don't recognize the cat and I tell her so.

later, I call my real mother up on the phone and tell her about the crazy lady
that came to see me at work, how sad it was that some strange woman
would fixate on me like that, would build up a whole history of my childhood based on
photos she had in her purse of a child that died so many years ago. the quiet
on the other end of the line tells me I should never have shared this story, that perhaps
my mother still wonders what her life would be like if something had happened to me
as a child, what she would do with all the anger, the grief
the freedom.

Hands Fold Like Dying Butterflies

in sleep, he screams to be put to use
I lie about what he does during the daytime: fifteen pairs of shoes in the closet
none of them fit either of us.

there are tiny phone numbers etched into the ceiling
quotes from Mussolini and Jim Jones in the sock drawer
pictures of the six million dead in a shoe box under the bed. I know who he is

I reject his past, I reject his status, I pretend
that nothing existed before we were married. I reject
the walls of hunger between us, how useless

our life together must seem to someone like him.

Printed in the USA
CPSIA information can be obtained
at www.ICGtesting.com
LVHW080228071023
760085LV00102B/1347